THE NEW RULES OF RECRUITING

D. ZACHARY MISKO | TODD WHEATLAND

THE NEW RULES OF RECRUITING

Kelly Services
999 W Big Beaver Rd
Troy MI 48084
USA

Copyright © 2013 Kelly Services, Inc
All rights reserved, including the right of reproduction in whole or in part in any form.

FOREWORD

Will you catch the wave and ride on its crest, or be dragged under by its force because you paddled out too late?

OK, that's a bit harsh. Nothing wrong with some drama to get your attention.

And let's be clear: We hope you're paying good attention. There are plenty of recruiting professionals out there content to do things the same way as before because by and large, it's still working alright.

We wrote this book because we feel the recruiting landscape has changed drastically, and many are still walking around with a mix of amusement and contempt for their peers who've embraced tools like social recruiting, content marketing and culture branding.

We're pretty certain (well, okay, we're totally certain but we don't want to come across as bullies) that those same colleagues will eventually use those tactics to rob you of the most valuable candidates—those knowledge workers critical to gaining a competitive edge in today's talent economy.

We aren't going to assume you're convinced. Far from it. We are going to explain many things that may seem only peripherally related to the New Rules of recruiting, but trends you need to understand in order to apply them:

- We'll talk of knowledge workers—those smart, high-value workers most global companies are racing to attract. Knowledge workers drive innovation, discovery and competitive advantage in today's economy—and recruiting them is your most critical role in the years ahead.

- We will also study Generation Y. Millennials are representing an ever-higher proportion of the workforce, and their expectations and communication style will shape the future of recruiting—and the way you do your job.

- We'll review the basics of why the way you used to do your job won't cut it going forward. In particular, we'll review why certain advances in technology are changing the rules of recruiting. You'll find out that far from sidelining your job, new technologies are putting you in the critical position of supporting your organization's core strategies.

- And finally, we'll dive into the New Rules—the evolving technologies and media tactics you'll need to add to your recruiting playbook. There's a lot to cover!

FOREWORD

We're not going to reveal the New Rules in this foreword because we need to be sure you understand why we're applying them. But let's make one thing clear: There's never been a more exciting or demanding time to work in recruiting. For professionals willing to rethink how they work each day—and take on new responsibilities outside of their comfort zone—this is the time to join, to ride the crest of the rising wave.

CONTENTS

PART 1
UNDERSTANDING HOW WE GOT HERE

1. You used to be your resume — 13

Resumes—long the calling-card of professionals everywhere—are on their way to extinction. Sophisticated search technologies and social channels offer recruiters unprecedented access to information, but leveraging these new tools requires a whole new way of thinking.

2. Recruiting the rock star employee — 25

Developed economies depend on knowledge workers—professionals with advanced technical and problem-solving skills. Trouble is, knowledge workers are a fast-evolving breed. Global companies eager to attract these competitive assets must adapt to their professional needs and work style.

3. Millennials and the transformation of work 35

Those born in the 1980s and later—also known as Generation Y—have indelibly marked the workplace, like it or not. Millennials want to work for organizations with a strong vision and corporate culture. With Gen Y maturing into professional roles, the tactics recruiters use to engage them must mature alongside them.

4. Remind me what we're doing again? 45

What do knowledge workers and Millennials have to do with new advances in recruiting? Everything. When the candidates you seek to hire are in high demand and are accustomed to using technology—particularly social media—to navigate their professional lives, you need a brand new playbook.

5. Social goes both ways 55

Social media is arguably the most significant disruption to the recruiting field. It's considered among recruiters and HR professionals by turns as a gift and a curse. Social media offers hiring companies unprecedented access to personal and professional information—but there's a catch. Candidates have access to the same universe of information to weigh future employers. Believe it or not, this newly empowered job candidate is a good thing for everyone.

CONTENTS

PART 2
THE NEW RULES: BECOMING THE FUTURE OF RECRUITING

6. The New Rules about building a positive employee experience   **65**

As a recruiter, your job is about to get bigger. Much bigger. Rather than filling positions in a one-off, tactical fashion, you're now also responsible for ensuring all potential candidates—even 'passive candidates' not yet ready to apply for a job—have a positive experience.

7. The New Rules about using social media   **73**

Let's study the complex array of social media and content sharing sites, and how recruiters use them. Remember, using social media is more 'gutsy experiment' than 'well-planned route.'

8. The New Rules about crafting relevant content   **91**

What's the use of social media channels if you have nothing to say? Along with building an online network, begin thinking of what useful information you have to share with it. Leave the sales pitch behind. In your new role, you're an educator.

9. Conclusion   **101**

10. About the Authors   **103**

UNDERSTANDING HOW WE GOT HERE

YOU USED TO BE YOUR RESUME

Remember your first resume?

It was a thing of beauty, a rite of passage, something to revere in all its crisp linen goodness. And it promised to unlock your professional future.

For decades those of us in the recruiting field relied heavily on what may now seem a quaint relic. If a candidate didn't get an interview, the resume was likely the culprit. Conversely, if a resume mapped out the right combination of experience and pedigree, an interview was nearly guaranteed.

It simply doesn't work that way anymore.

'In fact, many of the world's biggest and most sought-after companies no longer use resumes as a significant part of the hiring process. Automated tools, like applicant tracking systems, apply technology to screen large volumes of candidate—but for progressive companies it's just one element of a much more involved short-listing process. And there's good reason why: The resume is but a blunt tool when assessing whether a job candidate will succeed at a given company. In most cases, it is a linear and somewhat boastful march through a candidate's educational and job history, capturing little of a candidate's work style, soft skills and motivations. And it is decidedly inept when assessing how an individual will fit into the culture of an organization.

You may argue an interview can overcome some of the shortcomings of resumes, but even interviews only offer a limited snapshot. Some of the most brilliant and suitable candidates on your shortlist have surely failed to make the cut because of a one-off, poor interview performance, or simply because their personality didn't mesh with the interviewer's. Former Google CEO Eric Schmidt once quipped, "You are going to have to deal with the odd people. Not every single one of these incredibly smart people is a team player… even if people don't want them around, we still need them."[1]

Now consider this: How many times has a new hire gone terribly wrong not because the candidate had the wrong skills and job experience, but because they didn't fit with the organizational culture? Beautiful resumes and flawless interviews simply do not guarantee great employees. HR veterans know this.

---

[1] Cortney Fielding, "Eric Schmidt Explains How Google Hires," *GigaOm*, May 2, 2011.

How Google hires

Google is famously reticent about its hiring process, but over the years we've learned a great deal about how it identifies and selects the very best talent on the globe. The key? Google seeks out information that reflects less what a person has achieved and more how they think and act across all facets of their lives. The company wants to discover what drives a candidate in their professional and personal lives.

Eric Schmidt, former Google CEO, says, "People are going to do what they are going to do, and you're there to assist them. They don't need me; they are going to do it anyway [...] At Google, we give the impression of not managing the company because we don't really. It sort of has its own borg-like quality if you will. It sort of just moves forward."[2]

Identifying this individual who will fit into the Google culture—someone who is self-driven to solve complex problems and innovate across every facet of their lives—can't be done with a GPA or resume. So is there really a better way to assess an employee for hire? If resumes are so flawed, what will replace them?

---

[2] Ibid.

> **Will the resume eventually cease to exist?**
>
> Not likely. Some careers in particular still rely heavily on the traditional resume. In highly specialised fields—like medicine and engineering, for example—a curriculum vitae still serves as a statement that a candidate has attained all the necessary qualifications—both educational and professional.
>
> But outside these specialized professional positions, employers will increasingly use tools and tactics that evaluate the person behind the catalogue of positions and skills.

THE TALENT ECONOMY CHANGES EVERYTHING

To say the resume is no longer an apt tool simply because it's one-dimensional is only part of the story. After all, we've long known that an autobiographical career history is bound to be imperfect.

Other important trends have changed the rules of recruiting and undermined the value of the traditional resume.

- We now live in a world where talent is the most fundamental and powerful basis of competition. Never have the stakes been so high for identifying, attracting and retaining high-value talent.

- New technologies offer unprecedented access to information about companies and candidates. Resume 'proxies', such as a LinkedIn profile, hold much richer information for recruiters and HR professionals.

- Beyond providing access to information, social media also disrupts the role of recruiters in the employer/employee relationship. A job candidate can uncover almost any job opening through a simple search, and discover how they are connected to that company through their networks. Social media essentially removes recruiters as the sole relationship and information broker in the hiring process.

- Job growth in advanced economies is heavily weighted towards roles requiring highly technical or advanced problem-solving skills. Despite high unemployment rates, these jobs remain surprisingly difficult to fill, and resumes are not well suited to unearthing these skills.[3] Not surprisingly, online professional networks such as LinkedIn are perfectly suited to this need.

- In the last three decades, employee tenure has decreased dramatically. The U.S. Department of Labor's Bureau of Labor Statistics, for example, reports that among older wage and salary workers (ages 60–64), the percentage with 25 or more years of tenure declined from 23.3 percent in 1983 to 16.6 percent in 2006. For those ages 55–59, 25-year tenure declined from

---

[3] "Help wanted: The future of work in advanced economies," McKinsey Global Institute, March 2012.

22.7 percent in 1983 to 17.3 percent in 2010.[4] Although the percentages vary significantly across global markets, the overall reduction in average tenure is a global trend. Resumes—with their focus on pedigree rather than projects and skills—are poorly equipped to market individuals with shorter tenures at dozens of organizations.

- In his highly influential model, *Early Bird Sourcing*[5], Lou Adler explains the rise of passive job seekers—individuals who are not actively seeking a new job but are still open to new opportunities. LinkedIn reports 44 percent of all working professionals fit this category ("Willing to consider a new job but not actively looking").[6] Social networks offer unprecedented access to this group, and recruiters need different tactics to engage them.

- Finally, companies are relying ever more on 'free agents'—a group we'll cover in more depth in Chapter 2. Free agents help companies fill high-demand skills with just-in-time, temporary labor. Accessing these workers requires speed and access to robust global networks. Again, that traditional resume simply isn't up to the task.

There is perhaps no company in the world that understands and leverages these trends better than **LinkedIn**. In their own words, here's how they describe what's behind this recruiting revolution:

---

[4] Employee Benefit Research Institute: Dec 2010; volume 31, no 12.
[5] *A New Perspective on Sourcing Top Talent - Eight New Ideas You Need to Consider,"* Lou Adler, July 8, 2008.
[6] *"Passive Talent: Not as passive as you think,"* LinkedIn infographic, 2011.

YOU USED TO BE YOUR RESUME

Over the past 100 years, there has been a fundamental shift in the way companies compete. Historically, the market winners were those who had access to capital and financing. With capital, you could build the biggest plant, make the largest IT investments, or run the most impactful marketing campaign. Capital was important because size, not speed, was how companies won. Today the basis of competition has switched, as technology and the global economy both continue to accelerate the rate of change for businesses worldwide. While in the 1920s and '30s companies could expect to stay in the S&P 500 for 65 years, by the end of the 1990s this tenure dropped to 10 years.

In a world where speed wins, talent is the critical asset. A high performing workforce can see what is on the horizon, reacting and adapting to the environment before the competition. Even in a world of high unemployment, high quality talent has never been in such fierce demand.[7]

How then do companies identify and evaluate candidates in a post-resume job market? If resumes offer only a partial picture—and an inefficient way to canvass a pool of candidates—how do recruiters use technology to uncover better information?

Relying on social tools like Facebook, Twitter and LinkedIn—as well as all the other channels through which candidates leave 'fingerprints' online—we as recruiters can now peer into the online life of a prospect. By following a candidate's online behavior, we can uncover their professional networks, skills, motivations and passions. Next time you sit down to write

---

[7] *"Welcome to the talent economy,"* LinkedIn blog, March 7, 2012.

a blog post, edit a wiki, update your status, connect with a co-worker or tweet your thoughts, think about that content as part of your own ever-expanding, dynamic resume.

Essentially, your 'content' online is your new digital resume—and you may be writing it without even realizing it. If this sounds futuristic, it isn't. It's happening right now.[8]

You may say, "Being able to see what people do outside work isn't exactly new. I've always been able to ask about extra-curricular activities in interviews." The difference is this: In the past, the job applicant (and perhaps a referee or two) gave testimony to their motivations and extra-curricular interests, embellishments and all.

Now employers have the ability to verify their story by checking it against online behavior. They say they're an avid marathoner? It's easy to find evidence of online run registrations and fundraising efforts. Paul Ryan found this out the hard way in late 2012 when he was applying for the job of US Vice President and falsely claimed to have run a marathon an hour faster than he really did–something that was easily disproved online.

Someone claims they're passionate about design? It's a very simple check for guest blogging efforts, comments on design media sites, and collections on Pinterest or any number of other social channels. There's a claim that someone's well connected to attorneys specializing in pharmaceutical patent law? Their professional network can be checked to verify it.

---

[8] Rachel Emma Silverman, "No More Résumés, Say Some Firms," *Wall Street Journal*, January 24, 2012.

Your [exposed] social life: How privacy and recruiting will evolve together.

There's little use in thinking about public versus private, or professional versus personal in the way we used to. People can lock down their social profiles and delete errant tweets, but when employers go looking and find no activity in the online realm, they'll wonder why. The relevance and transparency of social media and the internet have changed the rules of recruiting.

Depending on the role, the organization and the market, employers increasingly want to get to know job candidates— including their online behavior. They'll expect activity in this space.

Our own research[9] into the thoughts and behavior of some 168,000 people worldwide shows that almost one-third of people now believe it is essential to be active on social media in order to advance their careers. Unsurprisingly, Generation Y are the most likely to be active online for career development, and those in emerging markets are particularly focused on it as a career-tool—more than half of respondents in the Asia-Pacific region regard social media activity as essential for career advancement.

---

[9] "When World's Collide: The Rise of Social Media for Professional and Personal Use," *The Kelly Global Workforce Index*, Kelly Services, June 12, 2012.

For better or worse, everyone's personal and professional self is documented through their online content and behavior.

While some may not realize it yet—and the ground rules for ethical and legal behavior are still being established—this massive source of information offers incredible new powers to employers, helping them choose new employees who have the right skills (of course) but also the right work style, attitude, passions and networks. If someone is the right person for a particular job, what they say and do online will align well with what the company is looking for—be it adventurous, analytical, opinionated or risk-taking.

For HR executives, recruiters and hiring managers, these new technologies are a powerful source of information and competitive advantage. But it's not as simple as just 'turning the switch.' Leveraging these evolving tools requires new recruiting strategies, organizational processes and niche talent. Ready to get started?

Yesterday, you were a resume. Today you're something else entirely.

Professionalism and social media

If it's true that potential employers can find out about someone based on their online activities—and vice versa—what's the right way to behave?

First and foremost, online activity should not be a sales pitch. Just because employers can see a person's social media tracks does not relegate them to live in a paranoid bubble. As any social media guru will remind us, when engaging online—be authentic. Everyone will edit, just as they do in real life, but their conversations should be an extension of their offline activity.

After all—those ideas, prejudices, views, and ways of working and interacting that don't fit with an organization's goals or ideals—will surface eventually (often far quicker than we'd like). In the past, people left their personal life at home when they came to work. Increasingly, there's less of a line between the two. Like-minds will gravitate towards each other and if we can skip the getting-to-know-you part (or at least make it a whole lot easier), we might just improve the way we make our matches.

In many ways, this new era requires little more than the advice your mother would give: "Be yourself." It's not about fitting in so much as finding where you fit. And that goes both ways—employees and employers will increasingly need to express who they are, contradictions and all, to find where they belong and with whom.

02

RECRUITING THE ROCK STAR EMPLOYEE

You most likely picked up this book because you're suffering a common ailment: an ever-growing difficulty in finding and attracting the right talent to work for you. The lack of qualified, talented and willing employees is a growing affliction for global organizations, and here's why:

The world's biggest economies have undergone rapid and seismic change in the past few decades. By the mid-80s, China and India began to shift gears and seriously mobilize their massive population for economic growth. They began to attract blue-collar jobs away from western economies and this forced a ripple effect across the globe. By the mid-90s, the European Union was well on its way to becoming an economic region, and despite all the complexity that has ensued, it now has a vast workforce that can move with increasing ease across borders to access employment.

The talent economy: Key terms

The 'talent economy' refers to the idea that companies will increasingly rely on talent (not capital, not scale, not cost containment) for competitive advantage. That puts recruiters and HR professionals in the position of executing on a mission-critical strategy. Never have the stakes been so high. To get started, let's understand some of the key terms associated with a talent economy.

Free agent: A highly skilled and experienced worker who provides their services and skills on a per-project basis.

Knowledge worker: A free agent or permanent employee whose skills are highly mobile and transferrable across borders. Key to higher-order tasks of organizations (e.g. engineering, product design and innovation, software development), knowledge workers are in high demand and short supply.

Workforce virtualization: When the deployment of a skill is not linked to or confined by a specific location (i.e. the skill can be delivered from one place to another without loss of impact). Work can be delivered from a virtual space that is not necessarily a workplace to the location that requires the skill. Workforce virtualization includes telecommuting, but also describes access to a virtual workplace, where all tools required for the role are available via networks. Using sophisticated technologies, employees can be monitored, coached and supported in more robust ways.

The world thinks of itself in regions rather than nations more than ever. It relies on cooperation, particularly economic cooperation across broader areas; increasingly labor forces will be regional rather than country-specific and—ultimately—global.

The reasons workforces are transforming to become transnational and mobile are four-fold:

1. Changes in one region affect others, so all economies need to adapt and fulfill their labor needs across borders.

2. Companies are more likely to be regional or global—they do business across borders, offering great opportunities for their employees to do so too.

3. Outsourcing to access cheaper labor sources—known as labor arbitrage—is now a long-established model across many industries.

4. Technology makes mobility possible. High-speed internet, mobile devices and cloud computing have made virtualization not only possible, but even more effective than traditional workstyles in particular skill areas.

SKILL REQUIREMENTS SHIFT AND CHANGE

As new industries and technologies evolve, they change the shape of entire economies. Suddenly, the skills required to fill vacancies are different, or the price businesses are prepared to pay for them fluctuates based on geographic, economic or technological changes. Outsourcing has fueled some of this tendency to look further afield for labor, but so too has the need to find larger numbers of people with skills in short supply.

Let's take the EU as an example. In 2000, the EU set a goal to become the most competitive and dynamic knowledge-based economy in the world. It's expected that by 2020 the share of highly qualified jobs in the region will increase from around 29 to about 35 percent. Other western economies are making similar moves, largely in response to the dramatic shift of manufacturing jobs to China and other parts of Asia and, to a lesser extent, Eastern Europe.

The growth industries and the overall shape of the EU economy reflects a continued shift away from lower-level production and service jobs, to a higher proportion of technical or 'knowledge' roles that require tertiary education. As developing nations eat further and further into the low-cost production jobs of developed nations, there seems little else for developed economies to do but to transform their workforce into something altogether different.

As the economies of the United States, some parts of Asia-Pacific and the EU take greater strides towards becoming 'knowledge' economies—where more of their workforce will be highly educated and have skills that will be in short supply all over the world—they are fueling the shift towards:

- Virtualized workplaces;

- Free agent work styles; and

- Knowledge work.

> ### A global, mobile workforce
>
> A study by IDC projected the worldwide mobile worker population—pegged at 1 billion in 2010—will increase to more than 1.3 billion by 2015. What's more—this change will be a major driver allowing companies to achieve greater levels of productivity.[10][11]

None of this has happened overnight. It's a trend building over several decades, but it has accelerated as technology has made tools and information accessible to a larger number of workers.

Those workers who describe themselves as 'self-employed' are a rising share of the workforce in many industrialized economies. In the United States alone, there are an estimated 10 million self-employed individuals, as well as almost 22 million non-employer firms (i.e. businesses with no payroll). These individuals are operating across a vast range of industries, with the greatest numbers in the services sector.

So, what does this all have to do with online recruitment? **Put simply, you're going to need to find more 'free agent/knowledge workers' from now on**—they're going to make up a larger share of every company's workforce. And unless you know the tools and places they use to find work, you're unlikely to capture their attention in significant numbers.

Welcome to the tough task of engaging the new 'rock star' employee.

---

[10] "Worldwide Mobile Worker Population 2011-2015," International Data Corporation, December 2011.
[11] "Making virtual work Business as usual," Deloitte, November 2012.

GETTING TO KNOW THE KNOWLEDGE WORKER

No longer tied to a desk somewhere within an easy commutable distance from a big city, knowledge workers in wealthy economies are growing in number. And as their ranks swell, the benefits of workforce virtualization and free agency become a known quantity on a mass scale.

As such, knowledge workers have penetrated all industries and extended across all nations. They include professionals in IT, healthcare, education, business consulting, engineering, science and agriculture.

Health services can be delivered via telephone and internet to remote places; design and some engineering services can be delivered far from site; and information technology and software development can be done almost anywhere. In recent decades, the discussion has been about how lower skilled jobs can be outsourced to developing countries—think call centers and IT processing centers—but now the ground is also shifting for knowledge work.

Whilst recession in the US and wage inflation in China has seen some lower-skilled manufacturing work start to flow back again, in the main, developed economies have lost huge numbers of low-value manufacturing jobs in recent decades. These have been replaced by positions that required the ability to understand and interpret information and generate high-value outputs. Most critically, however, knowledge workers fuel innovation and competitive advantage which in turn drives organizational performance. Knowledge workers offer specific expertise, and are frequently the agents of change.

Increasingly, this kind of talent prefers flexibility and a virtualized workplace. They look for the kinds of projects and employers that will grow and expand their skills. This focus on skill building and adaptability makes them even more attractive to other employers. And not surprisingly, it heightens their ability to set their own terms and work in ever-more flexible ways. As Thomas Friedman put it, these workers have redefined the orthodoxy of lifetime *employment* to one of lifetime *employability*.[12] Their emphasis is on obtaining the skills that will allow for lifelong learning and development as a pathway to long-term employability.

If it's true that an increasing proportion of your workforce doesn't need to be in a specific location to work, and these individuals are valued highly for their ability to drive innovation and creativity, then it makes sense to access the best of the best—not necessarily the cheapest or most conveniently located workers.

The more the link between work and location is eroded through advancing technology and the changing online cultures, the more flexible 'work' becomes. And this means that we have to do two things:

- Change the way we manage work and workers; and

- Change the way we find people to do what we need them to do.

---

[12] Thomas Friedman, *"The World is Flat,"* 2005 (Farrar, Straus and Giroux)

IT'S A NEW KIND OF MANAGEMENT STYLE

Workforce virtualization—where the worker delivers his or her skills and services from a location other than the employer's workplace—requires a new way of thinking about employees and the way they should be managed.

Organizations—and the management staff that lead them—must adapt to access talent across global networks. But recruiting these individuals will only succeed if the organization is ready to support them. Organizations vying for knowledge workers will also need to build and maintain frameworks, processes and technologies that support virtual employees and leverage their skills efficiently.

In knowledge-driven enterprises, managers are no longer the source of all wisdom. They are not required to know everything; rather, they are required to know *how and where* to access information and evaluate it. In these organizations, managers have a collaborative and enabling role. They must know how to get the best from their workforce, operating with teams to unlock creativity and innovation.

While that might seem like a lot to take in, there's a big connection here with online recruitment strategies. First and foremost, the knowledge workers—the top talent everyone really wants—will increasingly be found through social media and other online engagement techniques. This is their workplace, so there's no use thinking they'll be hanging about in recruitment companies' offices—or any other type of office for that matter. [We'll dive into discuss social media in Chapter 7.]

I'M BUSY. DO I REALLY NEED TO DO THIS?

For the majority of us, it's still hard to imagine that the picture of talent attraction and retention is changing as radically as it sounds. Many of us still go into the office most days. We can still find people the 'old-fashioned' way.

What's hard to grasp from one small desk (in just one company in one part of the world) is how much momentum the knowledge worker and free agent trends already have. In many ways, it's a kind of tipping point trend.

For a long while, it was a few forward-thinking and risk-taking people who were out there operating in this way. They were jumping from project to project and finding work while the rest of us were sitting back and thinking it all sounded a little too insecure and foolhardy. The global economic downturn of 2008 meant that increasing numbers of skilled workers turned to this work style out of necessity. In a relatively short space of time, it has become the preferred operating model of a large percentage of people with hard-to-find skills. Fifteen years ago, 25 percent of the US workforce were deemed 'free agents.' Today that number is 44 percent.[13] If you're not attuned to it, suddenly your competitors will be taking the talent you depend on, and you'll be chasing their tails.

---

[13] "The New Workforce: Insights into the Free Agent Lifestyle," Kelly Services, September 2011.

Want to attract self-employed knowledge workers?

Walk a mile in their shoes first. Think specifically how to:

- Frame work opportunities in terms of skill-building and lifelong *employability*. What new experiences can you offer the right person (once they've proved themselves)?

- Use language to sell a vision rather than a job. A distrust and disinterest in formal working arrangements is particularly high among this group.

- Join and participate in professional forums where your high-value free agents congregate; offer educational content like articles and webinars that advance their skills; and help them remain at the cutting edge of their field.

- Consider how projects can be split up into smaller pieces to make assignments more palatable to free agents and solo workers. If a project is too large, a free agent may have to excuse all other clients—a step most, particularly high-demand freelancers, won't consider.

MILLENNIALS AND THE TRANSFORMATION OF WORK

The influx of Millennials into the workforce has slowly and even painfully changed many rules of work that prevailed for Gen X and Baby Boomers. And even if you're pushing 60, this chapter matters deeply to you. Millennials, though still relatively young in their careers, are highly influential in shaping the future of work, connectivity and recruiting.

The Millennial mindset Gen Y is the first truly globalized generation of workers. They have grown up with the technologies that are responsible for creating borderless, globally integrated workplaces.

For Millennials, dealing with colleagues from different cultures and time zones is the norm. Younger generations know they need not be in the office to communicate and work effectively. And many of them will never be physically required to be in an office.

Generalizing about Generations

If you're confused by all this generational talk, you're not alone. The process of applying broad categories to hundreds of millions of people is by its nature flawed, however it has become a useful way of studying trends over time.

Because they are established through historical and cultural cues, different countries have their own versions of generations. In China, for example, generations are typically analyzed on a per-decade basis. In India, people commonly refer to the three generations since partition in 1947.

In the U.S., whilst there is much debate about specific start and end dates, there are typically five generations referred to, as outlined below[14]:

Born 1905-1924	The G.I. Generation
Born 1925-1944	The Silent Generation
Born 1945-1964	The Baby Boom Generation
Born 1965-1984	Generation X
Born 1985-2000	Generation Y / Millenials

---

[14] Kenneth W. Gronbach, *"The Age Curve: How to Profit from the Coming Demographic Storm,"* 2008 (AMACOM)

If Gen Y don't need to be in a single geographic location, they're unlikely to look for employment the way their parents did. Instead, they will look to their global networks—established over years of exploring the world and publishing their every move and thought via the internet—to find what suits them.

For the Millennial, the workplace is not solely about work; it is also a place for social interaction and shared learning. Likewise, personal time will increasingly be 'interrupted' or perhaps 'augmented' with more and continually evolving sources of information, including work-related ones. The way we live already keeps us continually connected with news and our personal interests. More and more of us have access to the internet wherever we go, and the line between personal and professional time is blurring.

For younger generations, this new way of working isn't the burden it has been for older generations, who compare it to what life was like 'before.' Younger people were born into this world—where mum and dad are 'always on', checking messages on Blackberries and iPhones, and outsourcing basic thinking to Google.

If this is how you've grown up, information gaps frustrate you. It's not so much that you have a short attention span or have technology-induced ADD, but rather you know what's possible—and when organizations choose not to provide it, you wonder why. You'll wonder, "What are they hiding?" Or more critically, "Is this an organization that will move fast enough for me and help me keep my finger on the pulse?"

> ### Millennials: A quick snapshot
>
> Businesses are under increasing pressure to attract talented Millennials; younger Millennials are now entering the workforce, just as Boomers are phasing into retirement.
>
> Millennials (also called 'Gen Y') have different attitudes, expectations and ambitions when it comes to their careers.[15]
>
> - They are more likely to see global experience as a positive differentiator in job selection and promotion.
>
> - They seek information and networks more broadly, using social media far more adeptly than many of their older colleagues.
>
> - Millennials are much more likely to allow work into their personal lives; they've grown up with mobile devices and have no qualms about using them to extend work into the personal realm.

Ultimately, this means that organizations are going to have to get more comfortable with providing more information about all aspects of their operation. They'll have to figure out how to make information available about things that were once only known by those who worked there. It's not that this is necessarily going to be sensitive information, but it's going

---

[15] Lance J. Richards and Jason S. Morga, *"Don't Manage Me, #understandme: Leveraging the Gen Y mindset and making it work within your organization,"* 2012, (Kelly Services)

to give potential employees a more complete insight into culture, decision-making processes and even structure.

The Millennial employee will seek out information most corporates haven't even thought about providing. This is going to be uncomfortable and older managers who belong to the 'remember how it used to be' mentality are probably going to wonder why on earth some of it is relevant. But it's going to happen—in fact, it already is.

SHOW ENGAGEMENT AND PROVIDE CONNECTIVITY

First and foremost, younger workers are going to look for employers that show they're engaged with, and connected to, online networks and information sources.

For Gen Y and those coming after, being connected is part of life. They'll no longer accept that when we go to work, we leave our private (i.e. globally connected) lives at home.

So, connectivity means many things to younger workers. It means having access to networks, information and technology that enables them to express themselves, communicate and find out what they need to know quickly.

And for employers looking to attract these workers, they had better get to grips with providing the information these potential candidates are seeking, lest they are overlooked by someone who does so faster and easier. Online openness reflects a more forward-thinking approach and a willingness to engage with employees' opinions and ideas—and this is how organizations are going to have to start working. Workplace culture, relationship building, and ongoing learning are all going to be more critical to retaining these individuals in the corporate world.

LIKE, ARE YOU SERIOUS?

Right now, most boards and management teams are still dominated by employees from the Baby Boomer generation. Older workers have different attitudes to work and the idea of a seamless 'third place' where work and one's private life converge sounds suspiciously like laziness.

All of that will change in the next five to ten years, by which time management teams will be dominated by Gen X workers (and even younger employees). The generations are different and they manage differently. The companies they lead will turn out to be rather different entities.

Gen X is known for several defining characteristics, but among these is the high importance it places on work-life balance. Leaders of this generation will be more accommodating and more understanding of the attitudes brought to the workplace by Gen Y and beyond. They'll understand the issues of connectivity and look to solve them rather than avoid them.

All this said, the task of recruiting and managing these latest (and future) entrants can seem bewildering, especially for those whose approaches are based on old notions of command and control. Gen Y brings a rich opportunity to challenge established notions, refresh practices and tap into new thinking. For many it's hard to let go of the idea that the way things used to be done wasn't really broken. True, it wasn't. But economies and regions are operating differently, and requiring a faster rate of change and adaptation from us all. Younger generations are just riding this wave more effortlessly.

For the workplace of the next five to ten years, when upwards of four generations will meet and work alongside each other, there will be plenty of discussion about whether technology and its social media spawn is destroying or enhancing our lives. Regardless, we now work in the multi-generational workplace, and this requires us to provide trans-generational solutions.

Understanding the varying needs of the different generations—everything from communication style, workplace style and expectations, management techniques, and organizational structures—becomes critical if everyone's needs are to be met. When needs are met consistently, chances are—you work for a high-performing company.

Attitudes of free-agent Millennial knowledge-workers

If you're going to recruit them, you must know them. Let's again walk in another's shoes to understand what Gen Y professionals look for in work and life:

1. **Information is everywhere.** In fact, information is so ubiquitous that my job is as much to filter as to gather. I filter information by relying on my social networks, selected digital publishers and specialized aggregation engines that learn what I like and serve it up to me on my schedule.

2. **Online engagement is just a natural part of life.** If you're not 'on' you're missing out. An ever-increasing proportion of the opportunities and interests that suit me are found only online—and a growing subset of those things on phones only.

3. **Everyone does things this way, don't they?** If they don't, I haven't heard of them—and I certainly wouldn't want to work for them.

4. **My life is short and precious.** I don't want to waste time doing something that doesn't fulfill me. I certainly don't want to be like my parents, who worked day in, day out in a job they didn't enjoy, for a company they didn't like—and that didn't care about them.

5. **The world is my oyster.** I've worked hard and studied for a long time. I've amassed connections, information and knowledge – now I want to amass great experience.

6. **Like attracts like.** No matter how specific or niche my interest may be, I can find other people who feel the same way. People used to conform, now they converge. I have such easy and vast access to networks and opportunities that interest me, I don't have time or the inclination to pursue things that don't.

7. **Corporates are part of *my* world—they have to show me they care.** People need to have their say and shape the companies they work for and with. The old idea of 'doing what you're told' isn't going to work for me.

REMIND ME WHAT WE'RE DOING AGAIN?

So far we've established…

- Leading companies no longer rely on resumes to identify and research candidates. These linear, static tools don't serve us well in a hyper-connected, fast-paced world.

- Knowledge workers and Millennials often have very different expectations from their employers. Among other things, they are interested in virtual workplaces, flexibility, corporate culture, true values and a global perspective. If they are not already doing so, global companies that hope to compete will need to rewire their recruiting practices to attract these professionals in their preferred work styles.

- Companies increasingly value talent as a primary source of strategic competitiveness. Where corporate leaders once vaunted 'access to capital' or 'global scale' as key drivers of success, they now view talent management as a core driver of innovation and competitive advantage. The role of recruiting has never been more critical.

You may wonder, "Does this all really apply to me? Aren't these issues in the purview of the C-suite, not HR?" Yes, many of these changes are strategic in nature, and require C-level advocates. But it's equally important for recruiting professionals to understand these changes because your role is at the tipping point of massive change.

To understand this more, let's compare and contrast the old and new paradigms of recruiting:

Old recruiting paradigm

A senior role at Company ABC opens up. A recruiter looks through his/her established network and contacts a dozen or more possible candidates. The position is also posted through traditional channels (e.g. company website and third-party job aggregators). The recruiter accepts resumes and selects a short list for interviews. After much review and discussion, an offer is made to the most promising candidate.

In this example, we assume a few things:

- The recruiter has the information the candidate wants about the company and the position.

- The recruiter also has the network and platform a company requires to access a strong pool of candidates.

- Limited information is available to both hiring company and candidate about the other party.

In other words, the recruiter is a primary power broker, and intermediates the exchange of information and relationships.

Now let's look at the new paradigm.

New recruiting paradigm

- The job candidate has access to vast amounts of information about the hiring company from current and past employees through social networks. The candidate can also find out about competing companies (e.g. How does a competitors' workplace, culture and benefits package compare to the company in question).

- Similarly, the company can find out much more about the candidate. They will learn about what the candidate has published online in their area of expertise (and the quality of their ideas), how extensive their professional network is in their field (and the seniority of the network), their personal interest and passions, online testimonials, the reputation of the last company they worked for, and the names of colleagues that worked with the individual.

And access to information isn't the only thing that has changed.

High-value knowledge workers can now weigh many more factors in his or her decision. Your company's culture and values, whether the job can be performed remotely, the type and quality of people they will be working with, whether the position will offer access to valuable networking opportunities, and to what extent the job will build on his/her existing skills. Far from trying to show off skills and woo the employer, a high-demand candidate will interview the employer to ensure the position aligns with her/her personal values and professional goals.

In this new paradigm, the role of the recruiter is completely transformed. A recruiter—once a gatekeeper between a job candidate and a particular job—must adapt to a world where information is much more freely available. Far from vetting the credentials and background of a particular job candidate, recruiters are now often marketing their employer brand to attract the best and brightest talent.

And that's why we're here. The tactics you used even five years ago no longer serve you well. Time to learn the New Rules of recruiting.

GETTING THE ORGANIZATION ON BOARD

Depending on the kind of organization you work for, the reaction you receive when you begin talking about recruiting knowledge workers, satisfying influential Millennials and investing in social media may be mixed.

Before you sit down in front of your leader and announce that Facebook is the new Times classifieds, and that you'll be spending your time blogging and hanging out with 30-somethings in Google+ circles, think about it from their perspective.

Remember that in many organizations, CEOs spend little time (or at least less than most of us) behind a computer. In fact, many don't read their own emails or always make their own phone calls. To this audience, the idea that you'll be spending time on Facebook probably sounds about as professional as going to the beach during work time. These are gross generalizations—there are plenty of senior executives who 'get' social media—but this is what many HR and recruiting professionals are up against.

In some circles, social media still raises hackles and suspicions. Unless you get it right and deliver tangible results from the outset, you could face some serious opposition to change from the people who matter most.

So, to ensure you have your pitch down pat and can fully grasp the reasons you're sending your recruitment strategy out into the ether, here's a little backgrounder:

The other major reason for switching your recruitment strategies to something a little less 20th century is this: People don't work the way they used to.

There was a time (not so long ago) when you had to leave your house to find your soul mate, to find a home for sale or to buy a new car—you had to commit and put in effort right from the outset. Just as those times have long since gone for the real estate, retail and dating world, so too have they ended for employment. Like it or lump it, people are getting used to things coming to them. They're used to searching and comparing easily and, if they can, changing when things don't suit them.

Employees have largely embraced digital recruitment for many of the same reasons people have flocked to online real estate, auto listings and dating—it's easier. Life moves faster these days, or at least that's how it feels, and online recruitment tools have driven specific behavioral changes for candidates. Thanks to this technological evolution, employees can now:

- Quickly and easily access volumes of data and opinion about a company, project, or even specific senior employees without getting out of their chair;

- Broadcast their views/experiences of, or questions about an organization to a global audience;

- Connect quickly and easily with colleagues (present and former) and discuss career-related information across their networks—defying traditional barriers of geography.

Because of all these things, in its own unforeseen and perhaps even unintentional way, online recruitment has:

- Contributed to increased employee turnover;

- Increased the availability of temporary, project or freelance work (and our access to it across borders);

- Helped to globalize and virtualize work, and increased geographic mobility.

REMIND ME WHAT WE'RE DOING AGAIN?

On top of this, online recruitment has made it harder to keep recruitment of specific roles confidential, and it has increased transparency of turnover and salary information. Employees now have access to substantially more information about you as an employer than was available even five years ago. They can make more informed judgments without ever meeting you, and in many ways, their employment decisions are far more informed than they used to be.

In case you didn't catch that, it bears repeating. All this transparency and even loss of control is good; it means when someone accepts a position they are more likely to fit in.

OTHER BARRIERS ARE ALREADY GONE

The next reason you're changing your recruitment strategy is because people don't stick around in the same job the way they once did.

There used to be a fairly long and solid list of reasons to stay with a current employer. But a long tenure has ceased to be so important for either side. Many managers have shifted their expectations; they want people who are hungry to learn and embrace change. The perception of disloyalty, or jumping ship when things get tough, is no longer enough to keep employees in one workplace. Recruiters now see the upside of varied experience.

Another key reason for people to stay with the same employer used to be access to employee benefits—healthcare, technology like mobile phones and laptops, company cars and retirement schemes. Decades of restructures, outsourcing and the erosion of employee benefits have seen the impact of this drawcard decrease. In fact, well-paid temporary and contract opportunities are growing in favor. People can now see that a well-paid short-term proposition is sometimes a better alternative to a long-term position that may not be secure or that only offers a limited benefits package.

So, with these constraints largely eroding, the ability to look at every advertised job in the known universe with a few taps and clicks has opened up the job-seeking market even further.

THERE ARE ADVANTAGES FOR EMPLOYERS TOO

And there's good news in this evolution for employers too. While it's now much more difficult for companies to 'control' what is said about them externally, they too have greater access to information about candidates.

Not only can online tools enable fast, easy access to information about individual job candidates, it can also enable access to niche groups across all the traditional boundaries, including geography.

Employers now have the ability to read resumes online, sift through content the candidate has published, as well as access information on the people who provide references for them. They can vet and cross-check information in a way that was once labor intensive, if not impossible.

REMIND ME WHAT WE'RE DOING AGAIN?

IT'S THE NEW MASS MEDIA

With tenure decreasing and the unquestionable attractiveness of permanent positions waning, the online recruitment boom continues to add fuel to employee turnover. For some time, online recruitment was the preserve of younger employees and was skewed towards specific roles at the lower and middle levels of organizations.

How quickly things change.

There now remain few strongholds where online job boards and social media tools do not dominate. Older workers too are switching to online forms of recruitment. With more knowledge and experience comes more opportunity—both on- and offline. And social media tools that spread job opportunities via personal networks naturally favor those with more connections and more to offer.

When we consider the shortfall of in-demand talent worldwide, it's likely that the online battle for more experienced workers is only just beginning to heat up. Right when employers need their staff most, employees are gaining greater options and incentives to leave—and this is only likely to increase.

IT'S NOT 'NEW' PER SE—IT JUST GIVES BETTER ACCESS TO WHAT WAS ALWAYS THERE

For all the fear of change and the shock of the new, social media and other online recruitment tools just build on what we've always done. Social media connects us with someone who knows someone who has a colleague who does exactly what we're looking for and just happens to be looking for work. That person was always there, the chance of finding them was just lower. Social media didn't create anything new; it just supercharged the utility of what we already had.

SOCIAL GOES BOTH WAYS

The New Rules of recruiting rest on three basic premises:

1) Recruiting the most valuable workers—knowledge workers—requires us to behave as they do. This means leveraging social media and content sharing tools to expand our networks; acquiring more and better information; and engaging in a dialogue with potential candidates (even if those candidates are not being actively considered for a position).

2) As recruiters (and as HR professionals and hiring managers) we must move beyond tactical thinking. While we will still be responsible for filling individual jobs, we also need to create a positive brand experience for current and future candidates. What's more, we are now charged with engaging potential candidates long before they are actively searching for work. Much like marketers tend to a brand's overall position in the market,

recruiters now have an active role in the management of the employer brand.

3) Social media is a powerful tool that requires time to use effectively. The most social media-savvy recruiters began by testing the waters, and making many mistakes. As Aaron Swartz, the late founder of Reddit, explained in a talk entitled *How to get a job like mine*, "Assume nobody else has any idea what they're doing either. A lot of people refuse to try something because they feel they don't know enough about it or they assume other people must have already tried everything they could have thought of. Well, few people really have any idea how to do things right and even fewer are to try new things, so usually if you give your best shot at something you'll do pretty well."[16]

Why is social media so central to the New Rules? Social media presents clear advantages over other job-seeking avenues, including:

1. **Relevance:** Using social media tools, job seekers discover opportunities when *they're relevant*. Social media platforms have content engines to recommend jobs. Those recommendations—based on complex algorithms—relate to a candidate's network, other jobs they've applied for, and keywords in their digital CV, among many other factors. The list of jobs served up on a social media site could potentially be much more refined than any traditional job board could generate.

---

[16] Aaron Schwartz, *"How to get a job like mine,"* 2007.

2. **Credibility:** Job leads often come through either direct contact or someone one step removed—regardless, a trusted and connected source. A candidate is more likely to consider the position as a genuine possibility even if they're not actively looking.

3. **Ease:** Job leads arrive without much personal effort; candidates don't even have to spend time searching or setting up alerts, as is the case with more traditional online recruitment. Customized job listings are served up alongside their other social feeds.

4. **Aspirational:** Job leads via a contact or through a social media engine may connect non-traditional candidates with a particular job. While a candidate may not think to apply for a specific job, a member of their network may recommend them.

RELEVANCE

There is much made of the ability of the internet to create far greater access to highly targeted and niche audiences. The power of social media is about connecting interests. For the job-seeking market, this means connecting people with exactly what they're looking for, when they're looking for it.

CREDIBILITY

Social media discussions may not penetrate the wider world, but they have meaning and resonance to those listening because they occur within a trusted inner circle.

Both job opportunities and opinions about employers carry more weight when they come from someone we know. In fact, people would rather rely on the opinions of total strangers about a company or brand, than trust official messages from the brand itself. Positive and negative views about individual employers and jobs reverberate in this chamber, and have a high degree of credibility. It is increasingly rare for someone considering a work opportunity not to search online, seek input or share comments with others in their online network.

Hiring people through social networks also takes at least some of the guesswork out of reference checking. People already provide referrals online for colleagues, and if you trust and admire the person providing the referral, you've already improved the reference process exponentially.

Importantly, in the online space, you can identify a range of potential referees who have worked with the job seeker previously—beyond those 'soft' ones provided by the candidate themselves.

EASE

Like-minded individuals working together are more likely to be productive and avoid the culture clashes of those sourced from disparate and disconnected places. Finding and building cohesive teams and people with a genuine respect and affinity with an organizational culture takes a good chunk of the work out of making a new hire productive. It also reduces turnover and enhances what's already working.

ASPIRATIONAL

Active job seekers are only a portion of the candidate market, and as such, online social media is perhaps the most powerful way to tap into passive candidates who are not actively looking for work but may be swayed by the right opportunity. Encouraging online networks to pass on opportunities to colleagues they think may be interested and suitable can expand your talent pool exponentially, particularly for roles that might require talent and skills that are not easily measured in traditional ways.

If you're looking for someone with drive, ambition, ingenuity or the ability to work with little direction or supervision, testing that before they join your organization is going to be difficult. Finding someone who has already identified these qualities in a colleague is going to be a little easier—and perhaps more successful.

LIKE ATTRACTS LIKE

Networking is natural because we are drawn to people who have similar interests, and/or think and behave similarly to ourselves. It doesn't mean that we always agree, but it does mean that we gravitate towards those who demonstrate something we align ourselves with — whether a common interest, cause or point-of-view. And this is where the real power of social networks lies.

Once you've found a successful hire, you naturally want to find more like him/her. Doing so in the past required quite a lot of effort on the individual's part. Besides that, they may have known of someone but lost touch and be less inclined to bother them without really knowing if it would suit or interest them.

Those dynamics have changed. Like-minded people can connect in virtual spaces and indicate in a variety of ways to others if they're open to job suggestions.

Social networking is a natural behavior. It wasn't invented—it has just been channeled into ever more specific and measurable spaces. Now, recruiters and HR people must flex their own social networks to find candidates, but also understand more about how people connect and interact with each other online.

You can see more about what a person's network says about them—and if their interview, and all the other measurements you've put in place to determine their suitability for a role, really add up.

How likely is it, for example, that someone educated in Atlanta, who has three years of work experience with a large corporation, who does not read or share any tech-related news articles with their network, and who has no influential contacts in San Francisco, is going to be successful working at a start-up?

Sometimes, the way we see ourselves is rather different to how we really are. Sometimes we overestimate our abilities. Other times we underestimate them. Interviews are just one of the tools that are designed to uncover these biases, but now HR people have another tool to add to their list. Social media is a natural extension of people's offline social behavior. What we do there and who we meet is reflective of our work style and can offer insights about our abilities and our ways of thinking that other tools cannot.

Using online information to align a candidate and job

- Employee B applies for a financial analyst role with a large local financial institution. He is young and has little experience in finance, but claims to have a high interest in personal finance and says he's a fast learner with a curious mind.

- Employee B's grades and references are excellent, but the recruiter still wonders whether he'll be dedicated to his new field.

- Employee B's LinkedIn profile contains a link to a financial blog called *Out of the Red*. The blog is aimed at providing financial tips to young people just starting out in the workforce. It compiles a number of in-depth and complex news articles from specialist financial media, and translates these into easy-to-follow tips. Employee B has been an active commenter on blog posts over the last 12 months and shows he has a good grasp of the topics covered.

- Employee B's Twitter feed also features a higher than usual proportion of economic statements and links. He follows both mainstream financial media *(The Wall Street Journal)* as well as more arcane publications in personal finance and investing.

THE NEW RULES:
BECOMING THE FUTURE OF RECRUITING

06

THE NEW RULES ABOUT BUILDING A POSITIVE EMPLOYEE EXPERIENCE

In a world where talent is the new competitive capital, companies are racing to not only become the best in traditional areas like manufacturing, supply chains, customer service and branding. They're also vying to become the very best *employer brands*.

Recruiters play a pivotal role in remaking the employer brand. As agents in the engagement process with job candidates, recruiters can help ensure job candidates have a positive experience across the entire continuum of their communications with an employer. This starts with early stage awareness, through to final offers—as well as onboarding onwards (but that's another book).

Playing this role requires more sophisticated skills than ever. In this chapter, we will block out tactics for different aspects of positive employer experience; from the actual job-seeking process with your company, to 'pull marketing' strategies to raise awareness with candidates before they are looking actively for a new position.

THE ELEMENTS OF A POSITIVE JOB-SEEKING EXPERIENCE

Our colleague, Jillyan French-Vitet, has written and spoken extensively about what it takes for employers to rewire their hiring processes to emphasize a job candidate's experience.[17] French-Vitet says candidates expect greater 'collaboration' with hiring companies than they did in the past:

- Recruiters must be able to spell out what the hiring process looks like at their company. What can they expect, and under what timeline?

- Job candidates will want to check the status of their application during the process. You should have technologies that allow them to do so easily, in real time.

- Candidates will want information about what it's like to work for your company, particularly information about day-to-day work life. This need is often due to a desire to align personal values with the vision and culture of their employer.

- Candidates will want to know: What is the experience of professionals in my type of role? How do other employees feel about the workplace?

---

[17] Balazs Paroczay and Jillyan French-Vitet, "Packaging and Selling the Candidate Experience," *ERE*, Apr 3, 2012.

THE NEW RULES ABOUT BUILDING A POSITIVE EMPLOYEE EXPERIENCE

No longer are candidates content to send in an application and wait quietly to hear back. Technology has made it easier than ever to communicate with our colleagues, and job applicants expect the same easy connectivity they experience in other aspects of their lives. Gen X and Gen Y, in particular, are accustomed to high degrees of sharing, transparency and connectivity in the workplace, and employers must adapt their practices and processes to satisfy these new expectations.

But 'employer experience' is not simply about making the hiring process more comfortable. We've already seen that as a recruiter, you're now responsible for much more than the tactical activity of hiring talent for individual roles. As we've discussed in previous chapters, there is now a quiet but powerful group of passive job seekers—up to 44 percent of all working professionals. In many cases, the best candidates for a particular job are not those actively searching, but professionals who are already employed (and would consider an attractive offer to move).

Did you catch that? The group of candidates you're required to communicate with just grew exponentially. No longer are you only wooing high-value prospects for a particular open position, you're now engaging a much larger share of the workforce, and doing so at a much earlier stage of the hiring process. In fact, you're now actively engaging high-value talent who are not currently looking for a job, and for whom you may have no job available. No wonder recruiters feel so fatigued before even beginning!

Our talent economy—as any other economy—exists in a world of supply and demand. Today high-demand roles may be software engineers—

tomorrow, they may be product designers. But you would be remiss to leave product designers off your list of niche experts to engage with simply because they aren't a point of focus today.

Building awareness and engaging with all these cohorts—whether they are active job seekers in high-demand fields or 'tire kickers' in niche areas you follow—requires a broad set of strategies and tactics. In this environment, HR professionals and hiring managers must think of the candidate experience as much broader than the back-and-forth of active hiring.

Says French-Vitet, "From the moment the first connection is made, be it a click on a job site, an email or a telephone call, the candidate experience begins. So, as we begin to see each 'click', 'email' or 'call' as part of a deliverable, targeted experience, we can begin to make it worthwhile for both parties. Instead of a cost that nets often only a single filled vacancy, it becomes an investment and a measurable way to build talent networks for the future."[18]

BUILD A 'PULL' RECRUITING PROCESS FOR ACTIVE AND PASSIVE JOB SEEKERS ALIKE

'Push' and 'pull' strategies are concepts most marketers already grasp. The traditional media landscape, as with the traditional recruitment landscape, was all about 'pushing' advertisements towards the right target market in the hope that it would inspire them to take action. In the social media era, no matter what you're talking about, it's more about 'pulling' the right people to you, and having an effect that's more akin to 'below the

---

[18] Ibid.

line' advertising. To explain this a little further, we need to look outside recruitment for a minute.

In the traditional marketing sphere there was a clearer differentiation between 'above-the-line' activities and 'below-the-line' ones. A television or print advertisement for example, was usually what's termed 'above the line'. It was an overt call to action to a mass audience and asked customers to call or visit once they'd seen it. Below-the-line activities are more subtle and speak to niche, specific and targeted activities that build brand awareness—and may not even be focused on achieving sales right away. Sponsorship activities such as the naming rights of an event or stadium are one example—there is no specific call to action, but it's part of a bigger picture of advertising activity that raises awareness of, and interest in, the brand. It will hopefully lead to sales later on, but with below-the-line activities, awareness is enough to start off.

If we apply these same ideas to online recruitment, we can begin to think about different channels as above-the-line and others as below-the-line— and invest in them accordingly. There's still the need for advertisements about specific job openings, but there's also the need to target and engage very specific networks over a longer period of time even when vacancies do not exist.

Instead of 'pushing' out direct advertisements to your target market and asking them to contact you, much of your online recruitment activity will be focused on awareness and relationship building.

Social media and online recruitment strategies are about putting the right information out, even if it's not about a particular vacancy or role, and building brand relationships that attract and convince the right people, over time, that you're worth working for.

> If someone is willing to engage with you before you have a vacancy to offer, they might offer a whole lot more loyalty and staying power than your average respondent to a job ad.

THE NEW RULES OF EMPLOYEE EXPERIENCE FOR RECRUITERS

○ **Be transparent about your workplace:** Not long ago, candidates' questions focused almost exclusively on the particulars of a job. Now job candidates want to know exponentially more—and they have the ability to find out most of it through the web. Among the issues they take interest in:[19]

- **Employer branding:** What's the reputation of the organization, what are its values and culture, and how does it engage with the community? And beware: Your branding must be authentic to your candidate's lived experience. Candidates will try to align your branding with their own experience to verify the message.

- **Facts, figures and data:** Candidates will seek out information about your organization, as well as competitors', in forming a decision. A profitable and growing organization will reassure, a company hiring for a role to support downsizing and restructuring will not.

- **Hiring process:** The hiring process will communicate how well organized and transparent a company is, or how bureaucratic and rigid it is. The hiring process also shows off your organization's trustworthiness and the degree to which it embodies its stated vision.

---

[19] Ibid.

○ **Invest in best-in-class technology to deliver a seamless candidate experience:** Believe it or not, your technology (e.g. your application tracking system, website, etc...) may be a candidate's very first impression of your company. These interfaces deliver a powerful message about how well you 'walk the talk' of your stated values.

○ **Every employee is a recruiter:** While you may be among the few people who are paid for recruiting, every employee your job candidate comes into contact with is personifying your brand. What's more, certain employees in your organization who may not be employed as recruiters have a powerful role to play in sharing their networks for talent sourcing. When you ask your employees to help you source talent, offer them tools to do so. Consider crafting messages they can release through their social networks (see the example from Salesforce.com in Chapter 7).

○ **Monitor your reputation online:** Pay close attention to online chatter about your hiring process and workplace. Social channels can be an excellent source of (free) market research about how well you manage job candidates' experiences—something too many organizations fail to monitor.

○ **Don't ignore your website's career pages:** Your website may no longer be the first place people go to find out about your business, but even so, it should be absolutely reflective of your brand and the talent you're trying to attract. If not, all your other efforts may be in vain.

07

THE NEW RULES ABOUT USING SOCIAL MEDIA

Even those among us who've embraced the brave new world of recruiting are feeling understandably circumspect—and perhaps even a little suspicious—about the evolution. While the world screams "social media revolution!" many are left scrambling, wondering how to put the pieces together without putting our businesses under increased pressure, or opening it up to new risks.

The question remains: How do we as HR professionals, recruiters and business leaders leverage and navigate this new recruitment landscape? After all, we still have to deliver actual results while we learn new things. We can't go off experimenting with social media strategies only to find our business cracking under the pressure of vacancies and high turnover.

Before we discuss 'how' let's detour briefly to talk about 'why.' What exactly is the role of social media in recruiting? And why is building your social network so critical?

UNDERSTANDING THE MECHANICS OF SOCIAL MEDIA

Social platforms are like relationship engines, allowing you to meet and communicate with a network many times larger than what could be accessed using traditional means.

But even talk of simple *scale* misses the point.

We've already agreed that in this new world of recruiting, you're not solely focused on transactions (e.g. fill job A with candidate C). As a recruiter, you're now a strategic asset—in charge of attracting high-value knowledge workers at a time when talent is the differentiating competitive advantage in global enterprise. And knowledge workers network and consume information through their social channels. Why?

Connecting with information and people through social networks is efficient. Platforms like LinkedIn, Facebook and Twitter use complex algorithms to recommend people and content you are likely to find interesting based on whom you already know and what you already read. Think of these as your personal *consigliore*, pointing you to people and ideas you may be missing.

Now consider the reverse: Your professional profile online and any content you publish (e.g. tweets, blog posts, whitepapers, etc.) will gain credibility and visibility through the size, activity, influence and composition of your social network.

Let's repeat that because it's a critical concept to understand: When you update your status on Facebook, for example, only a fraction of your network will see that update.[20] That's because if you had to scroll through every update from hundreds of friends, your 'feed' of information would be unwieldy. Facebook—just like most other social networks—makes a decision about how important you and your ideas are to each member of your network based on various aspects of your history. Who is in your network, how influential are they, how often do you publish online, how 'sticky' is your content (is it republished or commented on), and so forth.

Remember in Chapter 1, we spoke about how your behavior online is now in the public domain? Well it's more complicated than that. Your behavior online also tells the social sphere how much you *matter*, and whether those social algorithms should put your profile and your content in front of others. If social networks are like relationship engines, the degree to which you actively participate through those networks is simply a way to prime that engine.

This second half of the book is all about how to prime that engine, and maximize your reach and influence as a recruiter online.

Let's begin with an inventory of the social and sharing platforms out there.

---

[20] Nick Westergaard, *"Social Media: How to make Facebook's algorithm your friend,"* The Gazette, September 26, 2012.

Online job boards

At first, job boards existed alone in this new, recruitment parallel universe. They were one-dimensional tools where posts were searched using keywords and location filters and applicants would simply submit their resumes via email or online forms. In many ways, they were simply digital classified ads.

While in retrospect job boards don't seem particularly revolutionary, their effect was. For the first time, candidates could access a massive collection of vacancies in a single search. Assuming he or she knew where to look, a single candidate could now access virtually every public job vacancy in the known universe without leaving their desk. The dominance of particular job boards and their affiliates in different countries provides access to job opportunities across borders at incredible speed. Neither recruiters nor paper classifieds could hope to match that.

Online job boards are now the dominant way that people find work in virtually all parts of the world, outpacing other avenues such as direct hiring, referrals and traditional print advertising. More than one-quarter of employees (26 percent) gained their last job by using online job boards; It is the single largest recruitment tool globally, followed by 'word-of-mouth' referrals (22 percent).[21]

---

[21] *"Kelly Global Workforce Index 2011"* Kelly Services.

Job boards—now well into their second decade of operation—continue to grow in number and there are key, dominant players in every market. There are also niche sites that allow access to specific skill-sets and candidates.

Social networking sites

Job boards have given way to a more powerful capability, and online social networking tools are rewriting the rules of traditional resumes, as well as the way people look for work.

Tens of millions of users join global professional networking sites like LinkedIn every quarter. LinkedIn announced in January 2013 that its membership had reached 200 million users, spurred on by growth in non-US markets including Brazil and India.[22] But LinkedIn's growth does not tell the whole story. Rival sites exist in every developed economy and their popularity should tell us something fundamental about human behavior: Yes, we are social creatures, but we're social because it serves our individual and collective interests.

The simple power of social media is harnessing the natural human desire to connect and form communities with common interests. For LinkedIn and its admirers, popularity stems from its ability to connect individuals looking for new and better work opportunities with other professionals who can help them either directly or through their networks.

---

[22] "How CEO Marc Benioff turned salesforce.com employees into brand ambassadors," LinkedIn blog, December 2012.

How Salesforce.com uses LinkedIn for power recruiting:

Salesforce.com, a leader in customer relationship management software, leverages their employees' social networks to source knowledge workers. In December 2012, CEO Marc Benioff emailed his sales team with simple instructions:

To: # All Sales World Wide
Subject: Get Social and Spread the Word!

As we work to become a $10 billion company, we need to grow our world-class sales team—and you can help us do that by connecting us to amazing people like yourself. We've put together a few posts that we'd love for you to share with your networks. This is a great way for you to help us build our first-rate team and receive a nice referral bonus.

Post #1
Attention sales rockstars: salesforce.com is hiring! Join a world-class team at the most innovative company in the world. [Ping me if you're interested.] http://www.salesforce.com/careers/sales/

Post #2
salesforce.com is growing! Join our amazing team. We're hiring for sales positions across the board and around the world! Find open jobs here: http://www.salesforce.com/careers/sales/ – [reach out to me if you'd like a referral]

THE NEW RULES ABOUT USING SOCIAL MEDIA

> **Post #3**
>
> I'm in my #dreamjob at salesforce.com and we're hiring! Check out open positions here: http://www.salesforce.com/careers/sales/
>
> Aloha,
> Marc
>
> The strategy—which is deceptively simple—increased sales team referrals by 60 percent.[23]

Our own research suggests that about 25 percent of job seekers think of social media sites like LinkedIn as their primary job search tool. The reality is difficult to put an exact figure on simply because 'searching' and actually getting a job are two different things. It is increasingly difficult to know exactly which channel led to a new job, as a search typically involves many platforms. That said, there's no denying we are increasingly depending on social networks to recruit.

Recruiters have seen this wave coming for several years and have proven fierce adopters of social media. In the US, for example, 92 percent already use social media or are about to begin using social media for recruiting.[24] The thinking goes... if a recruiter's network is larger and more up-to-date than a competitors', that recruiter will have a natural advantage in finding the right candidate.

---

[23] Eliza Kern, "LinkedIn continues international growth, hits 200 million members," *GigaOm,* January 9, 2013.
[24] "Social Job Seeker Survey, 2011," Jobvite.

Blogs

As a thought leadership and relationship-building platform, blogs are powerful tools. A recruiter can use a blog to educate job seekers about finding jobs in their preferred fields, and position themselves as trusted agents in the process. Company blogs related to careers and hiring can be a strong outlet to share company culture, employee stories and related content. Blogs can also provide instant and valuable feedback on elements of your organization that would otherwise be difficult and expensive to gather. Using blogs in conjunction with other forms of social media can drive traffic to specific recruitment activities with relative ease.

Rackspace: Employer blogging done well[25]

Like many high-growth technology companies, **Rackspace** is in a perpetual and aggressive race to source high-talent developers, designers and engineers. The IT hosting company is 'fanatical' about serving customers, and wanted to ensure their company's unusual and fun culture was well understood by potential candidates.

"We should always keep in mind that the most engaged and longest lasting contributors to our organizations are the ones who fit within our cultures," Michael Long, former head of global employment branding initiatives, explains. "Our goal

---

[25] Bill Boorman & Sally Hunter, *"Don't Tell Me Who You Are: Show Me,"* KellyOCG, Oct 2012.

> should be to accurately depict ourselves knowing good and well that for the right person, we will absolutely be their best place to work."
>
> With that goal in mind, the company launched RackerTalent.com, a microsite and blog that highlights what it's like to work at Rackspace, from the professional to the downright quirky. The site includes a blog with 60 contributors from four continents, 'day in the life' videos and video interviews with employees. The goal: not to *sell* Rackspace but to capture the essence of the company as it is in the hopes of attracting future Rackers who have opted into culture they aspire to be a part of.

Review sites and Q&A forums

Job candidates use sites like Quora and glassdoor.com to research a particular job market, find more information about a specific company or interact with others about careers paths. Are sites like these social media? Yes, to varying degrees. Glassdoor is a great resource to see what former and current employees think of a company, but it doesn't help people have a conversation with anyone directly (users can post and comment on the site, though there is little direct contact and networking between users). Quora, on the other hand, is an excellent networking site. It's dominated by leaders in the tech field and connects people directly with the information and people that can help them with specific questions about almost any topic.

If your company consistently recruits expertise in a particular field, these types of sites are highly valuable to build networks of like-minded individuals, and source other experts and talent in particular fields. Quora for example is an excellent place to network with technologists, tech entrepreneurs and the technology industry investor community. Other sites have niche followings in different areas.

Content sharing sites

The number and variety of content sharing channels is expanding exponentially. Why does 'content sharing' matter to those in recruiting fields? Are you genuine about no longer simply being a tactician, searching to fill the next position on your list? Then you'll have to engage in more meaningful longer-term activity. Think of it this way: When you engage in a conversation with a friend, do you only speak to them in one place at a particular time about a single topic? No. Chances are that you meet them in various areas of your life, and talk about many common interests. The same is true of recruiters building relationships: No one social channel is going to satisfy all your needs. Building a relationship means sharing content and conversation in give-and-take interactions.

For recruiters, this often takes the form of sharing relevant information and education with your networks. And you should be finding multiple avenues or channels in which to do this. So far, we've only talked about social media, but content sharing sites are another great way to network and share with a group of like-minded individuals. And just be to be clear: content sharing sites often function a lot like social media sites, so don't get bogged down by the definitions.

Among the types of content-sharing channels to be aware of:

- **Video:** Users post videos—whether homemade or professional—to channels like YouTube or Vimeo to gain a larger audience. Companies may use videos to share 'day in the life' employee videos or publish interviews with key executives.

- **Photo sharing:** Sites and apps like Instagram, Flickr and Tumblr let users share photography and art with their networks. Others like Pinterest let you create a virtual pinboard of images that appeal to you. How does this relate to recruiting? These channels function as niche content sites. Recruiters can network with prospects, review candidate portfolios online, or share a company's images in the same way. Recruiters may also explore a candidate's hobbies and interests, adding additional dimensions to the person under consideration.

- **Multimedia platforms:** Platforms like SlideShare allow you to post content in virtually any digital format for others to view and comment on. SlideShare, which began as a professional site for sharing presentations, is a great source for reading professional thought leadership, sharing expertise, and interacting with others with common interests.

Finding the right sites to share your content will depend on how you want to be seen by prospective employers, as well as the kind of content you can generate. There are many possibilities, but addressing a relevant audience with beneficial content that sells your unique perspective is the key.

Webcasts and broadcasting portals

Webcasts (a streaming media presentation offered either live or pre-recorded) can be effective for offering professional development opportunities—and are used by recruiters to share information and offer education.

Hosting webcasts can attract market-savvy talent that is intent on continuous learning and development. If people have the motivation to learn and network in their own time, this is already a promising sign. You can also use participants' registration information to build ongoing relationships with talent who might be right for your organization, even if you don't have an opening straight away.

Social games and apps

Gartner predicts that by 2014, more than 70 percent of large global organizations will use at least one gaming application for a strategic or operational purpose; from employee training to health and wellness apps for employees. Using social gaming in recruitment is no longer uncommon. Among the most notable early successes was Marriott Hotels' *My Marriott* campaign, in which players take on the role of a kitchen manager in the format of *The Sims* or *Farmville* games.[26]

The tactic worked especially well for Marriott, which hoped to attract Millennials to careers in hospitality. L'Oreal and Deloitte are other early

---

[26] Barbara De Lollis, "Marriott tried Facebook game to recruit employees," USA Today, June 13, 2011.

pioneers in the field. On the whole, however, gaming is still a niche area that requires significant investment—as well as a good dose of creativity—to make it work. Next-generation recruitment-friendly gaming applications are already testing candidates' psychographics, problem-solving skills and creativity as they relate to organizational culture and specific job competencies.

Your own website

Your website is still a major port of call for candidates wanting to understand who you are, what your company offers, and whether they should be proactive about contacting you—so, it's important not to discount it as a channel. Think of your company website as a hub feeding your social outposts. When you publish information and education, you should do so on your own website, but you'll also distribute the same content through all your social and sharing channels.

THE NEW RULES OF SOCIAL MEDIA FOR RECRUITERS

○ **Experiment unabashedly:** Remember those words from Aaron Swartz and assume nobody else has any idea what they're doing either. Every recruiter using social media adeptly began as a Luddite, feeling their way through it just as you will. This is a medium where your best teacher will be experimentation.

○ **Put away your sales pitch:** Recruiters join social media networks to source job candidates, learn from thought leaders, and engage with 'influencers' who are well-connected. Always remember: Don't approach social media as a new arena to pitch your company and jobs. While this recommendation varies depending on whom you speak to, we typically say at least 70 percent of your interaction through social networks should not be about you. That means most of your social activity will be about sharing non-promotional information, commenting on the ideas of others, and generally *being helpful* to those in your network. We all know people in our networks who are constantly selling rather than engaging in an interesting conversation—and it's a turn off.

○ **Read voraciously:** The best way to learn how to operate through social networks is to become a *consumer* of content. At first you may simply browse blogs that interest you and stay abreast of what competitors are publishing and saying online. But before long, you'll need a system to find and regularly read the most useful content. Use RSS feeds—a system to alert you when specific websites update information—to stay on top of what thought leaders and competitors are saying. Instead of surfing to find all your favorite internet sites, an RSS feed aggregates all this content for you and presents it in a single newsfeed.

Depending on your comfort level, you may also try out other niche content aggregation and social media management platforms such as:

- **Flipboard**—aggregates content it thinks will interest you based on sites you specify and what your network is reading, and presents them in a magazine format on your mobile device (iPad, iPhone, Android). Flipboard is but one of dozens of content aggregation engines, though probably the most visually appealing of the group.

- **Hootsuite**—one of many popular social media managers—organizes your social networks in a single dashboard to align your message and monitoring across all your major channels.

○ **Explore and exploit niche channels:** The social web is a big place and you're but one tiny drop in the ocean. The best way to have an impact is to identify and exploit your niche. Ask yourself: What's your most valuable area of expertise? What specific category of talent are you sourcing? Once you define it, engage those networks and community groups that pertain to that narrow category. Joining a LinkedIn group about recruiting in general, for example, will likely be a time-waster. But if you are pinged each time someone on Quora asks about recruiting for high-growth startups in New York City (as an example)… you are much more likely to connect with the right people.

And don't forget to experiment with posting jobs on niche job boards. You can usually find them through influential blogs, social media sites or news sites in that niche.

O Use social media to monitor competitors and their top talent: Get to know the best talent working for your competitors. As restructures, mergers and leadership changes occur in your competitive landscape, pay attention to how this affects the talent they have. Often, these changes end up pushing talent out the door, or disrupting the motivation and loyalty of high performers, and can create genuine opportunities to engage with those individuals.

O Cross-promote your social channels: On all your websites and blogs, on every email footer, on each job listing, on all social channels, and within every piece of your content like whitepapers and blog posts, include links to the channels you're actively using.

O Connect your offline and online worlds: Attend relevant events in your industry and look for speaking and contributing opportunities wherever possible—and don't forget to connect with the event organizers, other speakers and attendees through your online networks right away while the memory is fresh.

THE NEW RULES ABOUT USING SOCIAL MEDIA

○ **Build a rich database:** No matter which tools you use, make sure you capture and store the contact details of the people you engage with along the way. Store contact information in your CRM of key influencers and 'persons of interest' you meet through social channels.

THE NEW RULES ABOUT CRAFTING RELEVANT CONTENT

We've discussed how employers deliver the right *experience* to job candidates, and why recruiters are now responsible for engaging both active job seekers and passive job seekers. And we've reviewed how recruiters use social media channels to multiply the reach and effectiveness of their networks.

There's just one thing missing now: content.

If you follow popular online technology media like *Mashable* or *TechCrunch*, you've heard the talk about this thing called capital-C Content. But what do they mean by it?

The boom in content has to do with the shrinking power of traditional media (e.g. television, newspapers and mainstream magazines… different media types which are all considered *content*), coupled with the growing influence and reach of small-time content producers like bloggers, niche media sites and all manner of self-publishers. We live in a world where high quality content—even content produced by small time players—can compete with content produced with big budgets and high production values. Think of it this way: If you have children under the age of 18, they are likely watching as much video content on YouTube as they do through broadcast networks. As they say in the ad industry: the 'battle for eyeballs' is on.

(You may be asking… are we still talking about recruiting? Yes, we're getting there!)

The obsession with content among brands is related to this shift in the structure and mix of media:

- Brands know that if they can augment or replace the media sites that typically speak to their customers, they will 'own' the media rather than 'rent' it (i.e. pay for ad space). Why pay a third party to rent a banner if a brand can own the site outright and control the discussion to some degree? More and more brands are jumping in to become publishers of content—either by collaborating with traditional media or trying to nudge them out of particular niche content areas.

- There's a compelling reason for this push to publishing. Buyers—whether B2B or B2C—often begin the buying process with an internet search. Whether they are looking for customer and expert reviews, buying advice or education about a particular topic, buyers use the internet to find this information. Rather than being at the mercy of third-party content, a company can ensure their brand and products appear as part of this internet search. The best way to do this is by publishing content.

- This shift we've described above—where brands develop content to engage directly with their customers—is a discipline called 'content marketing,' and it has become highly effective at reaching and converting customers.

- In fact, content has become the 'social grease' that powers social media. People use Facebook to talk about a new puppy or Uncle Tim's 80th anniversary party, but they also share articles that interest them and promote products they believe in. Companies can now use a combination of content and technology to increase their chances of being 'found' and 'shared' through social circles.

And here's where recruiters come in.

Content is a highly effective tool for recruiters to build and maintain relationships—particularly with those who are not active job seekers. Think of your social channels as a massive highway infrastructure. Content—whether blog posts, whitepapers, eBooks, podcasts or videos—are the vehicles you use to reach your prospects and customers through that infrastructure. Otherwise, your presence on these social networks is limited to the commentary you offer to other people's ideas.

In Chapter 7, we spoke about many types of content sharing categories. It's a fairly long list and we don't recommend taking on too much if you're just beginning. Some of the most straightforward content tactics to begin with are:

- **Blogging:** An old standby for content publishers everywhere, blogging is a highly effective tactic, with the barriers to launch quite low. Use a blog to educate your target market about your areas of expertise. But keep in mind, you should be answering your customers questions, not simply riffing about things that come to your mind. Be disciplined about the issues you'll cover—mining ideas from those niche sites you'll unearth based on Chapter 7. Great publishers always think from their readers' perspective, and you should too.

- **Whitepapers:** A whitepaper allows you to take a topic and cover it in more depth than a blog post. Again, think from the job candidate's perspective: What are their pressing questions, and how do those questions line up with your expert area? Choose a topic that's sufficiently narrow so you can cover it in depth. But don't let your whitepaper be more than six to eight pages in length; most reader simply don't have the attention to dive quite so deep. And just like blogging, stick to a schedule. Publish as many whitepapers in a single year as you feel you can produce well. For some, this may mean one per month, while for others, it can be as little as two per year.

- **Visual presentations or eBooks:** A presentation deck or eBook explores a single topic just as a whitepaper does, but the presentation is more visual in nature. Consider narrating your presentation in order to cut down on the wordiness of each slide. Presentations and

THE NEW RULES ABOUT CRAFTING RELEVANT CONTENT

eBooks are often easier for your audience to digest because they can scan for key ideas. These formats are an excellent choice only if you have a talented designer to guide your way.

- **Video:** The surge in smartphones and tablets has created a huge shift towards shorter, more visually engaging content. Video fits that profile perfectly – although it also tops most people's lists as the type of content they feel least comfortable producing. There are many ways to utilize video, from interviews to video blog updates to case studies and beyond. Although it's not technically a 'straightforward' content tactic, its huge growth rate means it's something you should be thinking about sooner rather than later.

As with social media, don't be shy about experimenting with content. But you should be careful of a few things:

- Never compromise quality: If you aren't capable of producing a piece that's well-written with original, intelligent ideas to share, don't bother. Poor quality is worse than no content at all.

- Enlist design and writing experts: You are likely to have a particular area of expertise to share, but you may not be a natural writer. Don't wing it. Hire the right people to ensure the finished product is polished, smart and uncompromising.

- Don't begin unless you can sustain it: A small handful of blog posts won't get you very far. Choose a publishing schedule you can live with, and stick to it. Consistency rules.

- Your content's value is based not only on the finished product (e.g. blog post or whitepaper) but how well you promote it through your social infrastructure.

> ### The Recruiter's Lounge: A blogging case study[27]
>
> Jim Stroud uses his blog to elevate his reputation, connect with others, educate his target audience, and simply soak up information about the changing world of recruiting. His experimental and quirky style gives him a highly original voice in a crowded field. What we admire is his willingness to take risks with content and be himself (no starchy, boring blog posts). For recruiters wanting to explore all the content formats available, Stroud is a great place to start. He produces blogs, podcasts, videos, cartoons, 'webisodes' and is widely regarded as a social media ninja.

---

[27] Jim Stroud's blog.

THE NEW RULES ABOUT CRAFTING CONTENT

○ **Become a publisher:** Create high quality and free papers, eBooks, and presentations; use them to engage people and share your strategy. This will go a long way to attract those who genuinely seek to be at the forefront of their field.

1. **Blog:** Use a company blog or specially created blog for a leader or topic relevant to your business to build your networks. Blogging is a simpler tactic to jump into, and done well is highly effective not only to build yourself as a thought leader, but to practice your new content and social media skills.

2. **Vary the medium:** As with all of the content you post, mix it up and keep it interesting. In this chapter we spoke of blogging, whitepapers and eBooks, but you may find certain formats appeal more to your strengths and style. Consider podcasting, webinars and video as well. Offering mutiple types of media means your audience can consume your content in the way that suits them.

3. **Host webcasts and other online 'events' and discussions:** Plenty of people still attend conferences, but many more access online content because of the ease and low cost. Put as

much effort into the presentations and conversations as you would any face-to-face forum—you never know who may turn up to listen.

◯ **Join the conversation:** Participate in discussion groups and comment on relevant content. After all, it's not entirely about the content you *create*, it's also about commenting and joining existing conversations. If you find someone with a great blog about a niche area of your business, look at who else is commenting—they might be the kind of talent you seek.

◯ **Re-use and Recycle:** Say you've written a well-researched and valuable blog post about breaking into the field of management consulting. Consider using that post to:

- Create a series of tweets about the topic, linking to your blog post.

- Publish updates to LinkedIn and Facebook with links.

- Create a short slide deck summarizing the ideas to publish on SlideShare.

- Use the post as part of a longer series about working in management consulting and use it to publish a longer whitepaper.

- Use it as an entry to guest blog for a media site with a larger reach.

THE NEW RULES ABOUT CRAFTING RELEVANT CONTENT

The point here is to ensure that for each activity you invest time in, you've created an 'echo effect' across all your networks by recycling content. If your original piece of content is of high quality and valuable to readers, it will stand up to this type of repurposing.

○ **Optimize your content for mobile and tablet:** More and more, professionals access content via smartphones or tablets, and it's critical any information you post is mobile-optimized. Don't just create a site, ad or blog and hope it will look ok on mobile; invest to ensure it works really well.

Also keep in mind, people are reading in smaller and smaller windows of time (e.g. commuting time). Ensure the information you offer is pithy and memorable even if someone is skimming.

CONCLUSION

In all aspects of our lives, technology is forcing evolution – much of it exciting, some of it confronting. As a result, we believe that the operating model for a recruiter has fundamentally changed.

In this book we've outlined the changes in the landscape – and shared our thoughts on the new areas of expertise and focus we feel are necessary for recruiters to excel.

We've talked about the ongoing boom in knowledge workers – those same smart, high-value workers that your company, your competitors and clients are fighting to attract. Knowledge workers create competitive advantage in the new landscape – and recruiting them will continue to be your most important role in the years ahead.

We've discussed the management challenge of the Millenials, who are on their way to representing nearly half of the workforce in developed economies. Their motivations, expectations and communication style will shape the future of recruiting – and as a result, the way you do your job.

And we've explored some core elements of the recruiter's role, and how the way many do their job just won't make the grade in the future. We've looked at technology's central role in these changes, and how far from sidelining your job, it's creating new opportunities to refocus and deliver value.

Finally, we've introduced the New Rules.

Transparency and interconnectivity means that your job is about to get much bigger. A recruiter's role is ever-more crucial as employer branding continues to grow in importance. Instead of focusing on one-off transactions, recruiters will be increasingly involved in shaping the employee and candidate experience for all potential future employees.

Social media creates opportunity alongside complexity, and more than ever, recruiters need to invest for the longer-term. Understanding your audience, and delivering relevant and original content, will help recruiters leave the sales pitch behind and be relevant in a networked world.

As with all change, these shifts represent real challenge. In the New Rules, we've aimed to empower Recruiters and show you a path to opportunity.

Good luck!

ABOUT THE AUTHORS

Todd Wheatland is vice president of thought leadership and marketing at Kelly Services, a Fortune 500® workforce solutions company, and a recognized authority on marketing, human resources and workforce issues.

Todd is a frequent speaker at events in the US, Europe and Asia-Pacific, and a regular contributor to industry publications including Mashable, Social Media Today, Chief Content Officer Magazine, DemandGen Report & B2B Magazine. A 15-year career veteran in the human resources space, his projects have been recognized by the AMI national marketing award, the Killer Content Awards, as well as the gold and platinum MarCom awards. He is a strategic contributor to the Corporate Executive Board's Marketing Leadership Council and co-host of the YouTube marketing show *Unsolicited Advice*.

Australian by birth, Todd lives with his family in Paris, France.

Draza Zachary Misko works with Fortune 500 companies throughout the world to develop and implement processes that improve and drive human resources and workforce solutions. Zachary is a senior executive board member of Best Practice Institute (BPI) and serves on the Human Resources Outsourcing Association (HROA) board, as well as the Latin America Regional Advisory Board for the International Association of Outsourcing Professionals (IAOP).

Zachary is published in several HR and industry publications and has spoken at over 100 conferences and events globally. He was named to the top 15 workforce and HR professionals under 40 in the US by Workforce Management magazine, and listed by the International Association of Outsourcing Professionals (IAOP)'s annual PowerHouse list of the top 25 outsourcing professionals globally. Zachary is also a certified Six Sigma LEAN expert.

A native of Wisconsin, Zachary and family divide their time between Milwaukee and Miami.

REFERENCES

Chapter 1

[1] Cortney Fielding, "Eric Schmidt Explains How Google Hires," *GigaOm*, May 2, 2011. http://gigaom.com/2011/05/02/eric-schmidt-former-google-ceo-how-google-hires/

[2] Ibid.

[3] "Help wanted: The future of work in advanced economies," McKinsey Global Institute, March 2012. http://www.mckinsey.com/insights/mgi/research/labor_markets/future_of_work_in_advanced_economies

[4] Employee Benefit Research Institute: Dec 2010; volume 31, no 12. http://www.ebri.org/pdf/notespdf/EBRI_Notes_12-Dec10.Tenure-CEHCS.pdf

[5] *A New Perspective on Sourcing Top Talent - Eight New Ideas You Need to Consider,"* Lou Adler, July 8, 2008. http://www.adlerconcepts.com/resources/column/newsletter/a_new_perspective_on_sourcing.php

[6] *"Passive Talent: Not as passive as you think,"* LinkedIn infographic, 2011. http://talent.linkedin.com/passivetalent/infographic2.html?trk-=blog.9.11.3

[7] *"Welcome to the talent economy,"* LinkedIn blog, March 7, 2012. http://talent.linkedin.com/blog/index.php/2012/03/welcome-to-the-talent-economy/

[8] Rachel Emma Silverman, "No More Résumés, Say Some Firms," *Wall Street Journal*, January 24, 2012. http://online.wsj.com/article/SB10001424052970203750404577173031991814896.html?mod=WSJ_Careers_CareerJournal_2

[9] "When World's Collide: The Rise of Social Media for Professional and Personal Use," *The Kelly Global Workforce Index*, Kelly Services, June 12, 2012. http://www.kellyocg.com/Knowledge/Kelly_Global_Workforce_Index/When_Worlds_Collide_-_The_Rise_of_Social_Media_for_Professional_and_Personal_Use/

Chapter 2

[10] "Worldwide Mobile Worker Population 2011-2015," International Data Corporation, December 2011. http://www.idc.com/getdoc.jsp?containerId=232073#.UP8SpeiiY-M

[11] "Making virtual work Business as usual," Deloitte, November 2012. www.deloitte.com/assets/Dcom-UnitedStates/Local%20Assets/Documents/IMOs/Corporate%20Responsibility%20and%20Sustainability/us_ds_workplace%20transformation_11292012.pdf

REFERENCES

[12] Thomas Friedman, *"The World is Flat,"* 2005 (Farrar, Straus and Giroux)

[13] "The New Workforce: Insights into the Free Agent Lifestyle," Kelly Services, September 2011.
http://www.slideshare.net/thetalentproject/the-free-agent-workforce

Chapter 3

[14] Kenneth W. Gronbach, *"The Age Curve: How to Profit from the Coming Demographic Storm,"* 2008 (AMACOM)

[15] Lance J. Richards and Jason S. Morga, *"Don't Manage Me, #understandme: Leveraging the Gen Y mindset and making it work within your organization,"* 2012, (Kelly Services)

[16] Aaron Schwartz, *"How to get a job like mine,"* 2007
http://aaronsw.jottit.com/howtoget

Chapter 6

[17] Balazs Paroczay and Jillyan French-Vitet, "Packaging and Selling the Candidate Experience," *ERE*, Apr 3, 2012. http://www.ere.net/2012/04/03/packaging-and-selling-the-candidate-experience/

[18] Ibid.

[19] Ibid.

Chapter 7

[20] Nick Westergaard, *"Social Media: How to make Facebook's algorithm your friend,"* The Gazette, September 26, 2012. http://thegazette.com/2012/09/16/social-media-how-to-make-facebooks-algorithm-your-friend/

[21] *"Kelly Global Workforce Index 2011"* Kelly Services. http://www.kellyocg.com/Knowledge/Kelly_Global_Workforce_Index/Social_Media_-_Networking/

[22] "How CEO Marc Benioff turned salesforce.com employees into brand ambassadors," LinkedIn blog, December 2012. http://talent.linkedin.com/blog/index.php/2012/12/benioff-salesforce-ambassadors/?trk=blog12.18.12

[23] Eliza Kern, "LinkedIn continues international growth, hits 200 million members," *GigaOm*, January 9, 2013. http://gigaom.com/2013/01/09/linkedin-continues-international-growth-hits-200-million-members/

[24] "Social Job Seeker Survey, 2011," Jobvite. http://recruiting.jobvite.com/resources/social-recruiting-reports-and-trends/

[25] Bill Boorman & Sally Hunter, *"Don't Tell Me Who You Are: Show Me,"* KellyOCG, Oct 2012. http://www.slideshare.net/ToddWheatland/dont-tell-me-who-you-are-show-me

REFERENCES

[26] Barbara De Lollis, "Marriott tried Facebook game to recruit employees," *USA Today*, June 13, 2011, http://travel.usatoday.com/hotels/post/2011/06/marriott-tries-facebook-gaming-as-tool-to-recruit-workers/174084/1

[27] Jim Stroud's blog. http://blog.jimstroud.com/

Made in the USA
Charleston, SC
29 April 2013